Blessed Are the Pure in Heart

Blessed Are the Pure in Heart

The Beatitudes

BERNARD HÄRING

Photographs by Ray Ellis

A CROSSROAD BOOK
THE SEABURY PRESS • NEW YORK

The Seabury Press
815 Second Avenue
New York, N.Y. 10017

Original edition: *Beatitudini: Testimonianza e Impegno
Sociale* © by Edizioni Paoline, 1975

English translation by Bernard Häring
Copyright © 1977 by The Seabury Press, Inc.
Printed in the United States of America

Library of Congress Catalog Card Number: 76-49766
ISBN: 0-8164-2125-0

CONTENTS

THE JOY OF THE LORD IS OUR STRENGTH

Christianity becomes a promise and a source of salvation for the world whenever people believe, with St. Francis and his brothers, that "We can live the Gospel, we want to live it and, of course, we must live it." Our faith is essentially a joyous, grateful acceptance of the saving truth, and our joy of faith is at the head of our commitment to it. Faith, or orthodoxy, without joy is not only unattractive; it can never spark a genuine Christian life of discipleship and service.

Perhaps we understand today, better than earlier generations, the words of St. James: "You have faith enough to believe that there is one God. Excellent! The devils have faith like that, and it makes them tremble" (James 2:19-20).

The Gospel proclaims that we are living in a favored time: that God guides us by his love and unites us in his presence. From this arises the moral imperative of the Good News. "The time has come; the kingdom of God is upon you; repent and believe in the Gospel" (Matt. 1:15). Prophecies have promised that God will gather us, give us a new heart, a new spirit, and that we can live

[9]

in this spirit. But the transforming power through which God's grace works in us to make us true disciples is the joyful trust that we can live the Gospel.

All of us are called to holiness. There is no monopoly on holiness; anyone who in the whole of life manifests the joy of the Gospel witnesses to this universal vocation. Some have received the particular charism of faith by which they can communicate to others their joy in the Lord and the conviction that everyone can live the Gospel of purity of heart, gentleness and total commitment to the good of their brothers and sisters. We no longer look today only to those in priestly and religious professions but also to men and women in the secular world for persons who are dedicated to the Gospel, who live it and help others to come to the same joy.

Prayer and meditation are expressions of this joy and of the longing to share it with others. Whenever this happens, people are truly gathered in the name of Jesus. Authentic religious communities, prayer groups and families that pray together give us an idea of how the promise of the prophets will be fulfilled: "I will bring them to my holy mountain and give them joy in my house of prayer. Their offerings and sacrifices shall be accepted on my altar, for my house shall be called a house of prayer for all nations" (Isa. 56:7).

Since Christian life is essentially the living of the beatitudes, followers of Christ can find special guidance for a life of faith and graciousness in the Sermon on the Mount.

The key to our understanding of the whole Sermon is in the Gospel introduction: "When he saw the crowds he went up the hill. There he took his seat, and when his disciples had gathered round him, he began to address them" (Matt. 5:1-2).

We could think that Jesus tried to escape the crowd by going up the mount, but this would contradict the whole of the Gospel and our faith. Jesus loves the crowd. He came as Savior of the world and shed his blood on Calvary for all of us. When he gathers his disciples around him, his heart goes out not only to them but to the crowd and to all people of all times.

We cannot truly find Christ and dwell with him unless we join him in his love for the crowd. But to join him in that love, we must come to know him as his friends did, as listeners who wanted to follow him regardless of the cost. Only when we know him intimately as the Emmanuel, "God with us," can we radiate in the world around us the joy, goodness, gentleness and mercy of the Lord.

As Christians, we cannot flee from people; yet we may and should sometimes retreat from the distractions and idols of the marketplace to listen more intently to Christ and to know him in his infinite love and compassion. Then he can send us, saying, "You are the light of the world."

Scientific study can never reveal the wonders of the Gospel of the beatitudes. Theological research and reflection are important, but the heart of theology and of Christian faith is the experience of Christ's nearness. He came from heaven for the salvation of all.

Jesus tells us, "I am the vine and you the branches. He who dwells in me . . . bears much fruit; for apart from me you can do nothing" (John 15:5). As for the outcome of our abiding with him, "This is my Father's glory, that you may bear fruit in plenty and so be my disciples" (John 15:8).

Through the beatitudes, Christ shares with us his knowledge of the attributes of the Father, so that we may be filled with gladness. When we abide in his love, rejoicing in his nearness and in his love for the world, then we too turn to the crowd with the same love and compassion as he did on the Mount of the Beatitudes.

In the following meditations, we first become fully aware that Christ, who is Beatitude Incarnate, is with us, and that we can understand the height, the depth and the beauty of his message only if we recognize him as the source of all joy and goodness. Next, we meditate on Christ's personal call to live with him the Gospel of the beatitudes. And finally, we think of the social dimensions of each beatitude, so that we may better fulfill our mission to be "light of the world" and "salt to the earth."

Lord Jesus Christ, we thank you for having revealed yourself to us as Emmanuel, "God with us." There is no greater joy in this world than to dwell with you, to rejoice in your friendship.

You have called us to join you, with so many others, on the Mount of the Beatitudes, to sing out the same joyous message you proclaimed to your disciples two thousand years ago. You want to share with us your love for the Father and your love for all people, and your joy in this love, just as you shared these treasures with your disciples and the crowds who listened to you when you walked with them in Galilee and Judea.

Lord, may I always reserve time to realize your nearness and to ponder your words. But make me equally conscious that I cannot stay with you or rejoice in your friendship unless I am as concerned for the crowds as you were, for you grant me these wonderful privileges not for myself alone but for the sake of your mission.

Lord, help us all to know that we cannot bring joy and help to the world unless we dwell with you, and that we cannot dwell with you and rejoice in you unless we accept our mission to be a living Gospel for your fellowmen.

Lord, here I am; call me.
Lord, here I am; send me.

HOW BLEST ARE
THE POOR IN SPIRIT;
THE KINGDOM
OF HEAVEN IS THEIRS

CHRIST THE SERVANT

For you know how generous our Lord Jesus Christ has been: he was rich, yet for your sake he became poor, so that through his poverty you might become rich'' (2 Cor. 8:9).

Before us stands Christ, the Son of God and Son of Man, rejoicing in his mission to be the Servant of all. "I thank thee, Father, Lord of heaven and earth, for hiding these things from the learned and wise, and revealing them to the simple. Yes, Father, such was thy choice. . . . Everything is entrusted to me by my Father; and no one knows who the Son is but the Father, or who the Father is but the Son, and those to whom the Son may choose to reveal him" (Luke 10:21-22). Turning then to his disciples, he

[17]

says, "Happy the eyes that see what you are seeing" (Luke 10:23).

Happy are we, too, if we see Jesus as the Servant of God and man, and want to follow him in his service. We can do this when we come to realize our need of God and, like Christ, know that our life, our talents and all we possess are from the Father to be shared in gratitude with our fellowmen.

Jesus grew up with Mary and Joseph, who came from the *anawim,* those poor and humble people who awaited the prophesied Servant Messiah who would care about the humble and the oppressed. Others might look for a conquering Messiah, but these *anawim* understood the secrets of the kingdom of God.

The first time Jesus spoke publicly in the synagogue at Nazareth, he read the great song of the Servant of Yahweh written by the second Isaiah: " 'The Spirit of the Lord is upon me because he has anointed me; he has sent me to announce good news to the poor, to proclaim release for prisoners and recovery of sight for the blind; to let the broken victims go free, to proclaim the year of the Lord's favor.' " Then, to the assembly he added, " 'Today, in your very hearing this text has come true' " (Luke 4:18-21).

In accordance with his Father's will, Jesus chose not only to live among the poor, the suffering, and sinners, but to be wholly dedicated to them and identified with them. His joy is in healing the sick, freeing the oppressed, proclaiming the Good News to the poor, for he came not for his own glory or to do his own will but to glorify the Father and to reveal the kingdom of God. Therefore the Father gave him a name above all names. He is called Lord because he is Servant of all.

On the Mount of the Beatitudes, Jesus turns his eyes and his heart to the crowd and sees there the humble ones who know their

need of God, and he promises them "the kingdom of heaven." (In his Gospel, Matthew conforms to a rabbinical custom which, out of reverence for the name of the holy God, substitutes the word "heaven" for "God." The "kingdom of heaven" is the kingdom of God: wherever God reigns as king.)

Only by the power of the Holy Spirit can we fathom the full meaning and beauty of this beatitude, personified in Christ himself. Christ is the "poor," the humble one who knows his total dependence on the Father. He is also the kingdom of God in person; God reigns in him. When the Spirit awakens us to this truth, we experience that "we can live the Gospel and want to live it."

By his poverty and his service, Jesus reveals to us the blessedness and richness of a life in the service of God and our fellowmen. Whoever follows him up the Mount and comes to know him as Servant has no longer any desire to possess, to dominate or to manipulate others; he wants only to honor the weak and to help them realize their own dignity as free human beings loved by the Father.

There is singular joy in sharing with others as Christ did. Anointed by the Spirit for his ministry, he knows that all he is and all he has is given by the Father, and that the utmost gift of his being the beloved Son is granted for the sake of the multitude; therefore his being Servant of all is a joyous and privileged expression of his gratitude to the Father.

FOLLOWING CHRIST THE SERVANT

Jesus made known his intention to serve the multitude when he came to be baptized in the Jordan with the humble sinners who, touched by the Holy Spirit, knew their need of God. And when the Spirit came upon him, the voice of the Father was heard, " 'This is my Son, my Beloved, on whom my favor rests' " (Matt. 3:17). If, in accordance with the grace and calling of our baptism, we follow Christ the Servant in thanksgiving for all that the Father has given us, then we shall receive the glad tidings, "Now you have become my sons, my daughters, my chosen ones on whom my favor rests."

The reign and kingdom of God becomes visible wherever people are moved not by fear but by that gratitude which opens us to the Holy Spirit and frees us from superficiality and petty concerns. Our life becomes praise and thanksgiving when we rejoice in using the gifts God has given us, knowing that we have received them for our mission. One who considers his capacities and possessions as something to be jealously kept for himself can never truly rejoice in the Lord or radiate that joy in the world around him. The truly spiritual person realizes also how much he is indebted to his fellowmen, and delights in returning to them what he has received from God through them.

When we rejoice in the Lord and experience the joy of sharing the Gospel and all the gifts God has given us, we do not require too many earthly possessions; we are happy in a simple lifestyle. If hardships come, they will not overwhelm us. A situation that might lead an unbeliever to desperation can seem relatively small to a true believer in comparison with the joy already granted and which awaits those who follow Christ. This, of course, does not preclude the enjoyment of material goods needed for a dignified human life, especially when we can help others with these resources for their human development and betterment.

SOCIAL DIMENSION

As Christians we are committed to the social dimension of all the beatitudes. Just after World War I, Pope Benedict XV stressed the relevance of the beatitudes to political life. We can think how different the consequences for the world might have been if the victorious and powerful nations of that time had mercifully granted all nations a chance to live in mutual respect and freedom.

As the law of the New Covenant, the Sermon on the Mount allows no narrow, individualistic interpretation. We cannot be disciples of Christ or live the beatitudes and at the same time participate in any attitude or action that contradicts the kingdom of love, peace, mercy and justice. Wherever God is reigning, the poor and unfortunate will never be exploited; there will be no collective egotism, no racism, bigotry or oppression. Everyone who really lives the beatitudes with joy and conviction is a sign of the kingdom of God, a light to the world that inspires hope and positive action.

Even where oppressors and powerful social classes are not yet converted to the kingdom, the beatitudes preached by Christ the Servant bring comfort and help to the humble. By preserving their inner peace and developing their own personalities in the goodness, compassion and concern for human dignity that the beatitudes teach, these people are truly blest and become signs of God's powerful grace. Indeed, they are a source of grace to all, for by their example they present an urgent plea to the rich and the thoughtless to be converted.

We cannot, however, limit the Christian message by using the Gospel to persuade the oppressed to accept passively their unjust status. Only those who are firmly committed to social justice can truthfully preach the Gospel. The spiritually mature, aware of their own need for God from whom they receive everything, will be ever conscious of their responsibility not only to share the Gospel and their gifts with their less fortunate brothers and sisters but also to join efforts with all who work for justice, truthfulness and respect for all humanity.

In the second century, a great theologian, St. Clement of Alexandria, wrote a book with the question, "Who among the rich will be saved?" He did not ask if the rich can be saved, for there is no doubt that the kingdom of God is offered to all. Rather, he asked what kind of rich people can be saved. His answer was clear: those will be saved who accept the message of the kingdom of God and therefore consider everything they possess, including their faith and their talents, as entrusted to them by the Father of all for the benefit of all.

This could lead to an extension of the first beatitude: "How blest are those who serve the poor and work to eliminate the conditions that oppress them." We can also say: "How blest are the mighty and rich who see their power and wealth as gifts and mission from the one God and Father, and therefore are free from lust for power and from desire to exploit or dominate others."

The first beatitude, then, means the reconciliation of the diversity of God's gifts with justice and brotherhood. This beatitude, proclaimed by Jesus the Servant, and shared by his followers, is not one among others; it is the foundation of all the beatitudes.

A great Orthodox Jewish thinker, Emmanuel Levinas, who miraculously survived Hitler's death camps, has the same basic vision expressed in this beatitude. He realizes that people can grow through suffering, but his main thesis is that a saving experience of God is granted to those who accept the poor coming from below as sent from above, and allow the poor to impose on them although they have nothing to offer but their claim as human beings. For Levinas, this poor person is sent from above and becomes the case that tests whether we can honor God, the Father of all, in the poorest of his children. Levinas' whole spirituality is based on the great songs of the Servant of Yahweh. And he dares to ask us Christians if we truly honor Jesus Christ as the One who embodied these songs throughout his life; do we recognize him as the Servant Messiah? It is a question we all must answer.

Lord Jesus Christ, I adore you in your poverty, for it reveals the richness of your love and your beatitude. Grant, O Lord, that we always adore you as the Servant of God the Father and the servant of all men, by being available to our fellowmen and by the humility and simplicity of our service to our brothers and sisters.

Free us, O Lord, from lust for power and from all desire to belong to a privileged class. Help us to love the poor and to appreciate their virtues. Enable us to love the sufferers and to lessen their miseries by the power of your love. In thanksgiving for your graciousness, let us never forget that they claim, above all, respect, love and justice as children of the Father. What they need most is the Good News, the knowledge of your name. Help us, too, to know you better, so that we can share with them this knowledge of you who came to bring the Good News to the poor as Servant of God and man.

HOW BLEST ARE THE SORROWFUL; THEY SHALL FIND CONSOLATION

JESUS CHRIST, OUR CONSOLATION

Here we meet Christ, the man of sorrows foretold in the songs of the Servant of Yahweh. "I have labored in vain; I have spent my strength for nothing, to no purpose . . . and now the Lord who formed me in the womb to be his servant . . . calls me again" (Isa. 49:4-5).

When Peter, touched by the Holy Spirit, professes his faith in Jesus as the Messiah, Jesus immediately lets his disciples know that whoever calls him Messiah must understand that he is the suffering servant of God and not the power-Messiah some people expected. "From that time Jesus began to make it clear to his disciples that he had to go to Jerusalem, and there to suffer much from the elders, chief priests and the doctors of the law, to be put to death, and to be raised again on the third day'' (Matt. 16:21). When Peter refuses to accept him in this role of man of sorrows, Jesus calls him Satan, a tempter, a stumbling block.

For this beatitude, then, we gather around Christ not only on the Mount but also under his cross, in grateful awareness that he has borne our burdens. ''Yet on himself he bore our sufferings, our torments he endured. . . . He was pierced for our transgressions . . . the chastisement he bore is health for us, and by his scourging we are healed'' (Isa. 53:4-5).

Jesus can console us because he does not turn away from us in the hour of suffering. He is with us and he listens. ''The Lord has given me the tongue of a teacher and skill to console the weary. . . . The Lord God opened my ears and I did not disobey or turn back in defiance. I offered my back to the lash and let my beard be plucked from my chin. I did not hide my face from spitting and insult'' (Isa. 50:4-6).

Christ is the servant who not only accepts the poor and the poor in spirit but allows them to impose on him. He allows even his enemies, like us who become his enemies by our sins, to impose on him. He is the supreme manifestation of the love and compassion of the heavenly Father, taking upon himself the miseries of a sinful world. He bears our cross and brings us consolation and redemption.

In his Sermon on the Mount, Jesus invites us to act in the same spirit. ''There must be no limit to your goodness, as your heavenly Father's goodness knows no bounds'' (Matt. 5:48); or, as St. Luke's version has it, ''Be compassionate, as your heavenly Father is compassionate'' (Luke 6:36).

Christ's is a blessed sorrow, born of divine and human love, a sacrament of the compassion of the heavenly Father. When Philip asks Jesus, "Lord, show us the Father and we ask no more," Jesus responds, "Anyone who has seen me has seen the Father" (John 14:8-9).

When, in the garden of Gethsemane, Jesus' suffering reached such intensity that he was bathed in a bloody sweat, "there appeared to him an angel from heaven bringing him strength" (Luke 22:43-44). The angel came, not to free him from his suffering but as sign of the Father's presence that strengthens him and opens to him the vista of final beatitude. He accepts, then, the cup of suffering from his Father's hands, knowing that it will be for the world the cup of salvation.

The promise and pledge of final beatitude is the risen Lord himself, who shows us the wounds in his hands, and his heart open for our salvation. They bring the good tidings that those who follow Christ even to Calvary will experience final consolation. Faith in the resurrection draws us and even compels us to gather under the cross of Christ. There, we will come to that deep and joyous God-experience which is at the heart of our faith in the resurrection.

GATHERED AROUND CHRIST

The famous ethologist, Konrad Lorenz, shows himself to be also a great therapist when he tells us that one of the *Eight Deadly Sins of Modern Man* is our incapacity to suffer with others and for others. If we are unable or unwilling to suffer in active compassion with others, we are also unable to share their joys, or even truly to rejoice at all, because one cannot experience deep joy without sharing it with others.

The measure of our capacity to open ourselves to blessed sorrow is our readiness to bear one another's burden. To express sorrow for others' unhappiness or distress is easy enough, but it is a kind of lie to express compassion if we are unwilling to suffer with them and for them.

There is a clear distinction between the afflictions that align us with a sinful and frustrated world and the sorrow that brings salvation. "The wound which is borne in God's way brings a change of heart too salutary to regret; but the hurt which is borne in the world's way brings death" (2 Cor. 7:10). For those whose self-centeredness locks them in their own little egos and separates them from loving human community and from Christ's own love, the Lord's beatitude is not available. Even sorrow for sins is not authentic unless we open our hearts to the misery and suffering of others.

The causes and quality of our sorrow mirror our own inner values. What are we revealing about ourselves, for instance, when we storm because we have been contradicted or misunderstood, or because someone is unwilling to dance around us, yet are undisturbed by the terrible suffering of millions of unfed and dispossessed people in the world, and the millions who are refused the most basic human rights? Unless we are concerned about others and willing to bear some of their burdens, we close ourselves to the joy that comes from God and leads to God.

The sorrow of "those who mourn," the bereaved whose sorrow has its source in love, carries within itself blessing and consolation. God is love, and where love is, God is. He consoles those who turn to him in thanksgiving for the love he has granted them, and gradually he opens for them new channels through which that love can flow out to the world in fruitful service.

There is, above all, the blessed sorrow that manifests the coming of the kingdom of God: the profound sorrow for sins which have caused suffering for others. Blessed are those who, after each sin, turn to God in sorrow and in trust. This was one of the practices of Pope John XXIII. "After each sin, I shall turn to God with an act of sorrow and great, great trust; and then I shall say, 'John, go ahead as if Jesus has given you a kiss.' " He was a man who could weep with the suffering and consequently could rejoice with the joyful. His was the profound consolation that arises from trust in God's consoling love.

When we turn to God with trust after each fall, we need not fear the misery of sin in our own heart or in the world around us. Our expression of contrition before the Lord makes us ready also to humble ourselves before the brothers and sisters whom we have hurt by our sin. Standing under the cross of Christ, our sorrow can never be because we have lost some advantage by our sin—that is our just due—but only because we have offended God and deprived our friends of the kindness and justice we should have provided.

SOCIAL DIMENSION

Every sin has a harmful social aspect. Whenever we neglect to do the good that we could and should do, we deprive the world of some light, trust and strength to which it is entitled. Whatever avoidable evil we indulge in increases the misery and slavery brought into the world by sin. But the sorrow that arises from God's grace and leads us back to Christ has an even greater social power. Pained by our sin because it has decreased the work of salvation, we renew our commitment to the Lord and to the world around us, resolving to make the best use of the gifts God has given us and thus to become, to the best of our ability, a source of salvation for others.

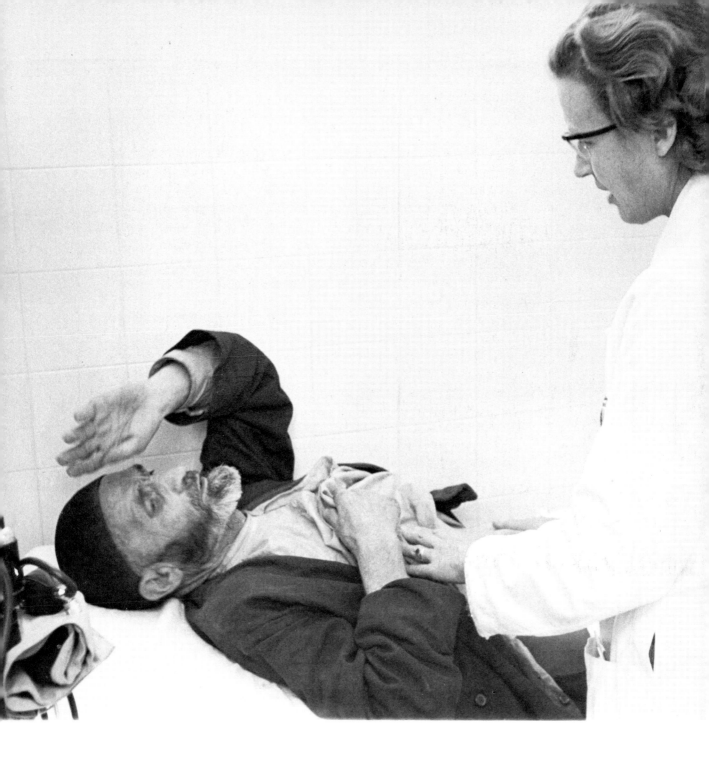

The new liturgy of the sacrament of reconciliation helps us to realize this social dimension of sin, sorrow, reconciliation and conversion. Our gratitude because God accepts us as we are, and forgives us, makes us willing to accept each other and to honor our common vocation to bear one another's burdens. The communal celebration of healing, forgiveness and renewal encourages us to confess our sins in both a sacramental setting and in our daily lives. If we meditate together under the Lord's cross, we cannot but commit ourselves to personal conversion and ecclesial and social renewal, as well as to whatever self-denial and suffering these may entail.

A deep faith-experience of the social dimension of each sin and of the terrible solidarity of sin in the world does cause us to suffer; but this suffering gives us an even deeper realization and experience of the solidarity of salvation, and leads us to recommit ourselves to this solidarity in Jesus Christ.

Wherever people accept the kingdom of God and are converted to Christ, many blessings ensue for the afflicted, the sorrowful, the lonely, the sick and imprisoned, for whoever is committed to the kingdom will never forget those who are particularly signed by the cross. Followers of Christ who have listened to him proclaim the beatitudes and have followed him to Calvary will never let their neighbor go hungry, or their old people live in desperate loneliness, or the sick and imprisoned go unvisited. Whoever abides with Christ, our Consolation, will spread the Gospel not merely by words but by that total witness that marks a person as a living Gospel. Blessed are those who, after being healed from their sins, give consolation to others; they will be a blessing for many who, without the Gospel, would live in darkness and despair.

The nearness of the Lord is our greatest source of consolation. We experience his nearness when we are gathered in his name for praise and thanksgiving, and in the desire to know him better and to follow him more faithfully. He has promised his presence to those who are consecrated to the service of his Gospel. If we are so consecrated, we will recognize him also, and especially, when he comes to us in the guise of the poor, the hungry, the sinner, the lost. There he is the crucified one but also the one who will be our Judge if we refuse him as our Savior. "For when I was hungry, you gave me food; when thirsty, you gave me drink; when I was a stranger, you took me into your home; when naked, you clothed me; when I was ill you came to my help, when in prison, you visited me. . . . I tell you this: anything you did for one of my brothers . . . you did it for me" (Matt. 25:24-40). Blessed are we if we discover this real though hidden presence of Christ crucified, who forces a decision upon us as to whether we meet him as Savior or as Judge.

As Christians, we suffer also from divisions in the Church of Christ, and from the sins of self-righteousness and group arrogance that cause them. But when we gather under the cross of the Lord, to repent together and to commit ourselves to pray and to suffer for the cause of Christian unity, then we shall know the joy of the Lord and shall, again and again, experience his consolation. Christ is with us through his Paraclete.

Lord Jesus Christ, great is my desire to have a share in the joy of your resurrection, and equally, to bring this joy and beatitude to my brothers and sisters. But so often I have failed in courage and in readiness to be with you on Calvary where you proclaimed, by your death, your new law of love, a love that is tested in suffering.

So I have not yet fully opened my heart to your boundless compassion for all men.

Forgive me, Lord. Heal me, for I have sinned. Let your Holy Spirit come upon me and cleanse me. Grant me a heart renewed, so that I may weep with the sorrowful and bring them consolation, as a part of my commitment to your Gospel of love and compassion.

In my daily life and in the celebration of your sacraments, open my eyes so that I may see with your merciful eyes as you looked to the crowd on the Mount of the Beatitudes.

Let us always be gathered around you, so that we may share your readiness to suffer for our fellowmen and thus become a living Gospel.

HOW BLEST
ARE THOSE OF
A GENTLE SPIRIT;
THEY SHALL HAVE
THE EARTH
FOR THEIR POSSESSION

THE GENTLE CHRIST

The first song of the Servant tells how gentle he will be: "He will not call out or lift his voice high, or make himself heard in the open street. He will not break a bruised reed, or snuff out a smolder-ing wick. . . . He will plant justice on earth" (Isa. 42:2-4).

Gentleness is the harvest of the Spirit, and Christ is gentleness in person. Anointed by the Spirit and filled with beatitude, he sees gentleness as the way to win hearts and to redeem the world. He had no wish to subdue the world by the sword; he chose instead the attractive power of kindness, patience, forbearance. As no one else before or after him, be believed that because we are created in God's image and likeness, we can be liberated and transformed by the love that comes from God and leads back to him.

In the crowd that listens to Jesus on the Mount of the Beatitudes are faces lined with care and suffering, and with sin. In them Jesus sees the face of all mankind and calls on his disciples to learn gentleness from him. He shows gentleness, and more, he radiates it. If we are truly with him, learning from him, we too will see the faces in the crowd and will become, in and through Christ, sacraments of his goodness, kindness, benevolence. "Come to me, all whose work is hard, whose load is heavy, and I will give you relief. Bend your necks to my yoke, and learn from me, for I am gentle and humble-hearted" (Matt. 11:28-29).

In Christ's appeal to his disciples and the crowd, there is no manipulation. His teaching liberates because it is gentle. By his life and death, by his word and radiant personality, he awakens in the hearts and minds of people the response of freely chosen discipleship. Whoever believes in him and abides with him will know the winning power of his goodness and will joyfully, gratefully and in total freedom follow him.

Again and again the Gospels show us Christ's gentle ways with all kinds of people. He wants the children to come to him, and indeed they must want to be with this gentle teacher who teaches by parabolic story and by praise of the good, rather than by threats and warnings of evil. He gently invites the blind man to come for healing whom others had tried to silence. He accepts Mary Magdalen so gently and trustingly that she becomes a new person. When he calls his disciples to come with him, and is confronted with their rudeness as they dispute who is the greatest among them, he shows boundless patience. He waits for them, calls them and teaches them by his own gentle word and example. When the priests and pharisees question him, he tries to convince them by his sincerity and quiet forbearance. And did he not give to his disciples—and to us in perpetuity—the gentlest of all commandments, "Love one another as I have loved you" (John 15:12)?

By Christ's gentleness he is the perfect sacrament of God's goodness. Through his deep experience of union with the Father, he experiences also his brotherhood with all mankind, and becomes for us our Way and our Light. If we as his disciples abide with him, learn from him and pursue his work in the spirit he has taught us, he can draw all people to himself and finally possess the earth.

GATHERED AROUND CHRIST

Jesus went up the mount and his disciples gathered around him. As believers, it is our privilege also to be with him there and to delight in the radiance of his goodness. But for the sake of the crowd we must remember that we are there to learn from him and to receive from him the gifts of gentleness, graciousness and nonviolence, so vital for our apostolate in the world.

Patience and gentleness have nothing to do with weakness, timidity or passivity. In the best Christian tradition, they are the noblest part of the virtue of fortitude. They combine the dynamics of love, benevolence and respect for others, and thus create that specific strength which gathers all the powers of heart, intellect, will and all of our passions for a firm commitment to the Gospel of justice and peace.

[41]

If we have learned from Christ, then we know that the way to attract people to his kingdom is by the same, gentle, outgoing love that drew the crowd to the Mount of the Beatitudes so long ago. Otherwise we dissipate in anger and frustration the precious energies needed for our service to our brethren. We are blessed if, through our benevolence, people can know that the kingdom of God is here: that Christ, exalted on the cross and exultant in his resurrection, is gently drawing them to himself by his love.

Whoever knows Christ as the humble servant will never attack others by offensive action or language. An old German proverb says, "Friend, you are wrong, for you are rude." Gentleness is a genuine sign that we are guided by the Holy Spirit and live in Christ's truth. "If you are guided by the Spirit, you will not fulfill the desires of your lower nature. . . . The harvest of the Spirit is love, joy, peace, patience, kindness, goodness, fidelity, gentleness and self-control" (Gal. 5:16-22).

In the four holy books of Confucius, we read, "The four greatest gifts which heaven has bestowed on wise people are benevolence, gentleness, justice and prudence." And it is noted that one cannot use patience as a tactic or learn gentleness before a mirror because these are the harvest of an interior benevolence and reverence. We can all rejoice that such insights, so close to the spirit of Christ, have been prompted all over the world.

Whoever has these qualities will spontaneously find the right expression in dealing with others. The New Testament often speaks of the necessity of "fraternal correction." However, it also tells us that whoever wants to fulfill this spiritual work of mercy must first learn from Christ's gentleness to act and react with profound respect and kindness. After having praised gentleness as the fruit of the

Spirit, Paul speaks about fraternal correction: "If a man should do something wrong, my brothers, on a sudden impulse, you who are endowed with the Spirit must set him right again very gently. Look to yourself, each one of you: you may be tempted too. Help one another to carry these heavy loads, and in this way you will fulfill the law of Christ" (Gal. 6:1-2). Here the centrality of gentleness is clear in the law of Christ. Without it we cannot express our saving solidarity with one another.

Great doctors of the Church like St. Albert the Great and St. Thomas Aquinas considered fraternal correction as one form of the sacrament of reconciliation, and set conditions under which it can acquire a sacramental significance as sign of Christ's gracious presence. And we do truly experience his presence when we offer this correction most gently and accept it from others in the same spirit. We are his messengers, the channels of his peace, when we join in prayer before him whose gentleness attracts us, heals us and forgives us.

The Second Vatican Council's text on religious liberty is significant in the light of this beatitude. It appeals to all believers to win over the earth for Christ and his Church by their witness of reverence and gentleness in the spirit of the Gospel. Indeed, only those who do manifest this evangelical graciousness can be said to be guided by the spirit of truth.

SOCIAL DIMENSION

The social relevance of the evangelical spirit of gentleness is obvious. Human relations on all levels and in all fields are often poisoned by bitter criticism, violence and humiliating manipulation because gentleness, the fruit of kindness and mutual respect, is lacking.

Disciples of Christ, who truly abide with him and want to follow him, have the distinct mission to carry this spirit into their milieu through their own benevolence. The many who suffer so terribly under neglect, manipulation, terrorism and other forms of violence urgently need these genuine disciples to create an atmosphere of mutual respect, and to work for social and economic structures that will foster it.

An important social contribution to this work is a constructive dialogue to promote healthy public opinion. Gentleness is the watchword here, for more will be gained by gentle persuasion than by rude or raucous arguments. Surely there is often need to express criticism, but it is more effective if we express our discontent or opposition by gentle, searching questions or with good arguments devoid of harsh words. Nor should we forget the effectiveness as well as the justice of expressing praise and sincere appreciation for what is fruitful in the other's opinion.

Not all ardent disciples of Christ have a political vocation, though it would be a happy development if the politically adept would use their charism for the reconciliation of nations and social classes. Yet all believers can and should influence their culture by bringing their values to bear on the political life of their community. Here again the spirit of gentleness and nonviolence is not only right but most effective.

Mahatma Gandhi, one of the great Christians of our era, had no distinct religious or institutional affiliation, yet he gave us a unique model of nonviolent action when he gathered his friends for meditation on the beatitudes and the Gospel of nonviolence. The

purpose of his ashrams and of his life of contemplation was to reach out for that perfect consciousness of union with God that leads to an equally conscious union with all mankind and with the whole of creation. This, of course, is the chief resource for strong, patient and convincing nonviolent action. Its strength in pursuit of social justice lies in the great power of truth: not truths discussed but truth itself, lived in solidarity with all people.

When hypocrisy and injustice must be unmasked, social justice requires courageous confrontation. It will be both nonviolent and liberating if we help those whom we have to reprove or oppose to discover their own inner resources of goodness and justice. If we believe in the almighty power of God's love and in the good will of most people, we can usually join hands for concerted action.

Those who find it hard to accept nonviolent action often refer to Christ's action in driving the traders from the temple. There is no evidence to prove that Jesus actually scourged anyone, although there is no doubt of his wrath at the misuse of religion; but none of us has his right to be an avenging judge.

If the Church remains a house of prayer and we all learn to adore God in truthfulness, our wrath will never be a useless explosion of energies. Instead we shall devote our positive energies to gentle but strong and sustained action for the liberation of all people in justice and peace.

Lord Jesus Christ, you not only spoke of gentleness to your disciples on the Mount of the Beatitudes; you have radiated this wonderful gift by your life, and continue to do so by the mission of the Holy Spirit. Let your Spirit come upon us so that we may become for our brothers and sisters visible signs of your gentleness and messengers of your truth. Free us from false confidence in our own strength, and never allow us to place our deepest hope in any form of earthly power.

Lord, teach us to be humble and of gentle spirit. When you invite us to gather round you and to rejoice with you, let us never forget the multitude who are oppressed, exploited, manipulated. Fill us with zeal for justice and true brotherhood.

Forgive me, O Lord, for so frequently engaging in useless dissent. I have failed to be an image of you. Too often have I tried to impose my own way of thinking on others when I should have first listened to them; and because of my lack of patient respect, what could have been a dialogue of faith degenerated into useless discussion. Thus I have missed occasions to win over those around me to the kingdom of your peace and your benevolent reign.

Send forth your Spirit and grant to us a heart renewed; grant us a new spirit of gentleness and nonviolent commitment. Lord, make us patient. Lord, make us gentle.

HOW BLEST ARE THOSE WHO HUNGER AND THIRST FOR GOD'S JUSTICE; THEY SHALL BE SATISFIED

CHRIST, THE NEW JUSTICE

The Servant of Yahweh foretells the justice that will come with the Messiah. "He will make justice shine in truth; he will neither rebuke nor wound; he will plant justice on earth while coasts and islands wait for his teaching" (Isa. 42:3-4).

What is this new justice, celebrated by the Servant, that neither rebukes nor wounds? To understand it we go to the One who hungered and thirsted to plant it on earth so that his heavenly Father would be honored and glorified by a more brotherly and equitable world.

So we gather around Jesus whose greatest desire was to teach this merciful justice which God manifested in him, and to see it planted in human hearts and reflected in all human relationships. It is the justice of God, the almighty Father who, after having created us in his own image and likeness, cannot abandon us to the misery of sin.

We could approach the matter of justice with some fear, for we know that, in strict justice, we sinners have no title to reconciliation or to reintroduction into the family of God. But God, in justice to his name as Father, cannot give us up. For his own name's sake, he is obliged to care for the weakest of his creatures. On this our hope and our salvation depend.

Christ, who makes visible the invisible God, perfectly mirrors his heavenly Father's merciful justice. His whole life and his death manifest it. True man and truly our brother, he has received from the Father the greatest possible gift, divine sonship. And because this gift to his human nature is bestowed for the salvation of all, Jesus feels obliged in justice to live and die in the service of his brethren. For their sake he hungers to establish the new direction of justice for all mankind.

He indicates this at the time of his baptism in the Jordan. John the Baptist is shocked to learn that Jesus wants to be baptized with the crowd, but Jesus responds, "Let it be so for the present; we do well to conform in this way with all of God's justice" (Matt. 3:15).

His baptism in water is but a sign and promise of the baptism in blood which he will receive for us on the cross. The blood of the new and everlasting covenant is the consummate expression of the new brotherly justice that he thirsted to bring to earth. Even on the cross he dispensed it, asking forgiveness for those who crucified him and promising the kingdom to the thief beside him. In fulfillment of the Scriptures, he said, "I thirst" (John 19:20).

If we, having followed him to Calvary, have learned to share his hunger and thirst for God's merciful justice for all, then we can truly be called his disciples and faithful members of his Church.

GATHERED AROUND CHRIST

Christ's most privileged disciple, the one closest to him, is Mary, his mother. From the moment of his coming she sings of the justice he brings: "The hungry he has satisfied with good things, the rich sent empty away" (Luke 1:53). Queen of the prophets, she tells of the greatness of the Lord who dethrones the arrogant and exalts the humble.

If, in dependence on the Holy Spirit, we gather with Mary under the cross, pondering all she has treasured in her heart, we will learn something of the intensity with which Jesus hungered and thirsted to plant on earth a justice that neither rebukes nor wounds. Then we shall free ourselves from petty worries and from our jealousies and self-centeredness, and will try to continue Christ's presence on earth, so that the humble may be exalted and the hungry filled.

Baptism brought us into the one great family of God where each, according to the gifts God has given him or her, cares for those in need. If we believe in the baptism of Christ and our share in it, we cannot accept our earthly goods, our talents or our special charisms as if they were ours for ourselves alone. We can receive them and use them in justice before God only if we serve first his needy children.

If we truly meet Christ in the celebration of the sacrament of reconciliation, we discover that the real sins are those against justice and peace among individuals and social classes, and we realize that we cannot receive the word of forgiveness if we refuse to test the sincerity of our hunger and thirst for God's merciful justice in our own relationships and concerns. In examining our consciences, we must daily ask: "Do I truly thirst for the justice that unites us all in mutual respect and in concern for those who need it most?"

SOCIAL DIMENSION

Of all the beatitudes, the social dimension of this one is most evident. Christ looks into the crowd and thirsts for a justice that far transcends the usual meaning of this word. God's justice is by no means a synonym for laws that preserve unjust privileges and the concentration of power in the hands of a few; it is a holy justice of love, mercy and basic justice for all. In this light we assess the problems of our day.

Glaring injustices abound, and to mention a few leaves out many others. But we can at least consider the humiliating punishments meted out to members of the oppressed classes for relatively small crimes while the powerful, whose clever crimes bring suffering to thousands of victims, receive strangely delicate treatment. And we can share the shame of a society which accepts and of the laws which legalize the slaughter of unborn human beings merely for the social convenience of those who refuse the consequences of their own willed acts. A society vilifies itself if it merely protects the rights of the selfish, the powerful and the vocal.

But to bewail injustices is not enough. As disciples of Christ we are committed to oppose all injustice by all the means at our disposal. Do we consciously concern ourselves with the basic right to full human life for those in the ghettos of our own city? Do we honor and help the unwed mother who, despite her human frailties, accepts in patience the responsibility for her own behavior? Or do we share in the injustices around us by our lack of action, by our self-concerned votes, our collaboration or our silence, inertia or cowardice? Do we not all need to say ''Mea culpa''?

Believers who have stood under the cross of Christ, Redeemer of the world, will understand the relevance of a genuine political vocation. An authentically religious politician can contribute greatly to the welfare of a state and to social and international justice. But political activity is marked by a hunger and thirst for justice only when it combines competence with absolute sincerity of motives and the courage actively to oppose unjust trends even when majorities or strong groups favor them. A former senator has said that his greatest political success was when he was beaten in an election because he had finally made it quite clear that he was opposed to all forms of racism.

On the national and international scene, a follower of Christ will never support or condone unjust terms for peace. He will firmly oppose any collective egotism that offers only unconditional surrender to those who must submit, or requires them to renounce their most basic human rights.

Today's society, and more likely the society of the next decade must confront organized crime and national and international terrorists who have no conception of justice. We surely need a trained police force to combat these evils, and we give due respect to the men who defend the lives of the innocent. However, to think that a strong police force and the death penalty are enough to resolve these problems is ludicrous. Along with the commitment of good people to building an atmosphere of respect for every human being, we need an intelligent approach that will remove, insofar as possible, the main causes of criminality and terrorism. The world needs disciples of Christ who have learned from him a merciful justice.

The faith that we celebrate in the Eucharist is a living and saving faith only if it prompts us to live justice in our families and in all of our relationships with others. If the awareness of our union with God is growing, so will our hunger and thirst grow to find appropriate ways, in cooperation with our fellowmen, to satisfy that hunger.

Some argue that immediate and effective action for social justice deters people from prayer and evangelization. But if we have truly felt Christ's thirst for God's justice on earth, we will surely understand better what constitutes genuine prayer, and will proclaim the Gospel in the way that he did on the Mount when he told how blest are those who help to plant on earth a justice that neither rebukes nor wounds.

Lord Jesus Christ, you have made visible your hunger and thirst for God's merciful justice when you prayed for those who crucified you and assured the thief by your side of your eternal friendship.

You have come to kindle the fire of love and saving justice. Grant, O Lord, that we may share your burning desire to see the Father's justice planted on earth. May we live the life of your most privileged children by going to meet those most in need of it.

[58]

Lord, liberate us from all selfishness, individual and collective. Free the mighty and the rich from a narrow concept of justice. Set us free from that concept that would have us serve only those who can repay us. Let us rejoice in serving those who have nothing to offer us but their need and their dignity as human beings.

Lord, make us grateful when we celebrate your saving justice. Make us vigilant so that we may discover the many opportunities to make known your justice to all people.

HOW BLEST ARE THOSE WHO SHOW MERCY; MERCY SHALL BE SHOWN TO THEM

THE MERCIFUL CHRIST

In the great prophetic tradition Mary sings, "His name is holy; his mercy sure from generation to generation toward those who fear him" (Luke 1:4-9).

We gather now around him who is sign and sacrament of his heavenly Father's presence in the world and whose whole life and death speak of the Father's mercy.

We can best understand this mercy in the light of God's saving justice, whereby his own name as Father is justified by all the manifestations of his mercy. His image revealed in Jesus Christ is of a God who is both holy and merciful.

The concept of God in Greek philosophy was of an immobile being who, because of his absolute perfection as first cause, could not be moved by mercy and compassion; these qualities were considered incompatible with his absolute sovereignty. But the revelation of God through the prophets and through his perfect revelation in Jesus Christ, his Son, is that of a God who *because* of his holiness and perfection is merciful without end.

Jesus not only speaks of the blessedness of mercy; he personifies it. Whoever sees him knows the compassion of the heavenly Father, and whoever knows the Father through Christ knows that mercy and compassion is the way of salvation.

Throughout the Gospels we see how wonderfully Jesus deals with sinners and restores them to a sense of dignity. How respectfully he meets the woman of Samaria who was known as a sinner! How kindly he assures the woman taken in adultery, "Neither do I accuse you," and sends her away healed! With what merciful eyes he looks at Peter who has denied him three times, swearing, "I know him not!"

Always his revelation of the Father is as the compassionate Good Shepherd foretold by the prophet Ezechiel: "For these are the words of the Lord God: 'Now I myself will ask after my sheep and go in search of them. . . . I myself will tend my flock, I myself pen them in their fold,' says the Lord. 'I will search for the lost, recover the straggler, bandage the hurt, strengthen the sick' " (Ezech. 34:11-16).

In the midst of his own suffering Jesus is more concerned for those who suffer with him than for his own anguish. "Do not weep for me; no, weep for yourselves and your children," he tells the women who mourn for him on the road to Calvary. And he prays for those who crucify him, "Father, forgive them; they do not know what they are doing" (Luke 23:34). Thus even in those dreadful hours, he was still teaching what he taught us on the Mount of the Beatitudes: "You must be merciful as your Father is merciful" (Luke 6:26).

When we have listened to Christ on the Mount, and seen him on Calvary, then we again gather around him who is the risen Lord. There we are reminded that all the splendor of the resurrection is given to him because he has so fully revealed the mercy of the heavenly Father.

OUR VOCATION:
TO BE A LIVING GOSPEL OF GOD'S MERCY

The one who stands closest to Christ under his cross is Mary, his mother. We honor her under the title, "Mother of Mercy." But our veneration is honest only to the extent that we, too, become images of God's own mercy as revealed in Jesus Christ.

The Church, of which Mary is the prototype, is a sacrament of salvation whenever she is the visible and attractive sign of the mercy of the Lord. Without fidelity to his mercy, neither the Church as a whole nor any of her members can be truly faithful to the spirit of any of God's commandments, nor can they live any of the other beatitudes.

The fear that some people feel about death is often the fear of the divine Judge. But we know how to prepare ourselves for a death that will be filled with trust instead of fear. It is simply to live the

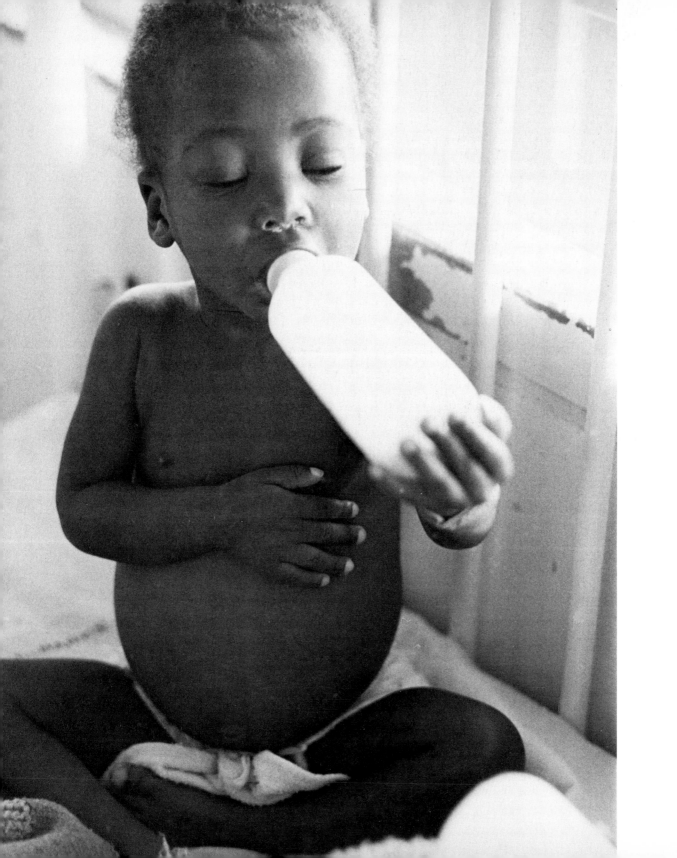

beatitudes; then we know that mercy will be shown to us. Salvation is an act of God's merciful justice; we are justified by pure grace. But final salvation also depends on our grateful response to the mercy we have received. Then Christ's gladdening news for the blessed who have shown mercy will be the final judgment. "You have my Father's blessing; come, enter and possess the kingdom that has been ready for you since the world was made. For when I was hungry, you gave me food; when thirsty, you gave me drink; when I was a stranger, you took me into your home; when naked, you clothed me; when I was ill, you came to my help; when in prison, you visited me" (Matt. 25:24-26).

Excluded from the kingdom of mercy will be those who, though they may have observed all the minutiae of the law, have dealt heartlessly with the needy.

In the celebration of the sacrament of reconciliation, Jesus especially proclaims his mercy and compassion for us, and offers his healing forgiveness. We receive it and are healed insofar as we, too, become apostles of healing forgiveness.

SOCIAL DIMENSION

Works of mercy have both individual and social dimensions. The Church as a whole and many religious communities are dedicated to the works of bodily and spiritual mercy. Long before governments undertook any of these works, the Church provided hospitals, orphanages and shelters for the sick, the helpless, the mentally ill, and the unwanted. To these have been added various assistance programs and aid to victims of natural disasters. The Church could not continue these works if it were not for those of her members who abide with Christ and learn from him the blessed-ness of the works of mercy. It is in fidelity to this beatitude that we appeal for vocations to the religious and priestly life, and for voca-tions among the laity dedicated to particular works of mercy.

Each one of us and each community has a special charism for at least one of the many aspects of mercy taught by Jesus. One who recognizes the suffering caused by loneliness will visit the old to brighten their dull days, to console them, to pray with them and to render modest services. Others, especially touched by the plight of the handicapped or deficient, will come to encourage them and help them toward their maximum achievement, and to give what assis-tance they can. Often just to listen is more important than material help: to let people know that someone cares about them, to assure them of their own worth, and even more to praise them for the lesson they teach and the inspiration they give by their patience and courage.

Many senior nuns and other retired people are now finding their greatest joy in an apostolate to the elderly and other shut-ins. When Cardinal Frings, Archbishop of Cologne, retired, he asked for ap-pointment as chaplain to elderly priests. Although nearly blind himself, he daily visited old and lonely priests, and by just being with them manifested his sympathy and appreciation.

There are other disciples of Christ who regularly visit prisoners who have no family or visitors: a beautiful vocation! The wife of a Protestant pastor has visited, every week for the past six years, a black boy who, since the age of twelve, has been confined in correctional institutions. Through her, he has gained confidence that when he is free he will be able to live responsibly toward his fellowmen. This good woman feels that the boy would never have

been imprisoned if his extraordinary talents could have found an outlet, and that when he is released from prison he will become a leading figure in our society.

Individual assistance to prisoners is surely a blessed work of mercy, but beyond that much remains to be done by pooling our efforts for the radical reform of our whole correctional system. If the healing forgiveness of Jesus were made visible there and in our whole society, then the hope for better opportunities in the economic and social world would encourage many unfortunate prisoners to look forward to responsible citizenship. Also needed are vocations to chaplaincies and to the particular social works involved in the correctional field.

The bishops of Germany have inaugurated a concerted action of assistance to developing nations. Its name, *Actio Misereor,* means action that expresses Christ's mercy. Just feeding the hungry does not suffice. They try also to help the poorer nations to cultivate their own talents and resources, which is one of the best ways to show mercy. It is a matter of social justice that the wealthy nations should share the earth's resources with the less favored; but whether for the sake of justice or mercy, it is the duty of believers to promote generous assistance programs for the least fortunate children of the one merciful Father.

If we believe in God's mercy then we must live it in our own lives and promote it in our own neighborhoods, our own nation and internationally. Only if we ourselves show mercy will God's mercy be shown to us.

We praise you, Father, Lord of heaven and earth, for having sent us Jesus Christ to be the great sacrament of your compassion-

ate love for all people. If all our lives were to become praise of your mercy, our whole earth would be transformed into a dwelling place of peace and joy. Let all our voices join with Mary's in praising your name because of your mercy.

Lord Jesus Christ, let our eyes be open, that we may see the crowd as you saw it, and thus learn to show mercy as you did to all our brothers and sisters. Free us from any tendency to judge our fellowmen, for you did not come to condemn but to save. Let us learn to become your image, you who are the Divine Physician, the Good Shepherd, so that the Father's name will be revealed to the world.

Lord, make us grateful. Lord, make us merciful.

HOW BLEST ARE THOSE WHOSE HEARTS ARE PURE; THEY SHALL SEE GOD

CHRIST, THE INCARNATION OF PURE LOVE

As his disciples, we are called to the Mount to meet Christ who has come to teach us how to love on earth as in heaven, that is, totally and with a pure heart.

Jesus' whole life and his death reveal the holiness of love between the Father and the Son, in the Holy Spirit. With the same purity of heart with which he loves the Father, Jesus loves us, his brothers and sisters. He is Love Incarnate, the Word who speaks God's love for us in total self-bestowal. Consecrated by the Holy Spirit to fulfill the Father's will in pure love, he shows by all his life that he has come not to do his own will or to seek his own glory but that of the Father.

The biblical concept of God's glory comes close to what we call purity of heart. God does not need his creatures; his majesty is absolute and stands alone. That he takes care of us and reveals himself to us is total gift, proof of the absolute fullness and purity of his love.

Because Jesus perfectly reflects the purity of the Father's love, he is glorified. He is the "Light of Light" while he is also the humble servant who gives himself to those who cannot repay him or who are unworthy of his love.

It is not we who initiate the love relationship with God. We respond to God's own initiative who first loved us although we do not merit it. This truth shines through all of Jesus' words and deeds, telling us that purity of love is a supreme attribute of God, wonderfully revealed in the person of his Son.

CHRIST, THE SOURCE OF PURITY OF HEART

Christ shares with us the purity of his love whenever we come to him with some sincerity and with a longing for greater sincerity in our commitment.

The marvelous promise of this beatitude is that "they shall see God": that even here on earth we can come to a blissful knowledge of God, a foretaste of the everlasting beatific vision.

God is love, and only those who have learned to love with a pure heart can have a blissful God-experience and receive that knowledge of God that bears in itself all beatitude. The saints and prophets longed to know God with all their affections, passions, intellect and will, but they also knew that they could not come to this kind of God-experience without purification of heart and mind.

Moses found favor with God, and Yahweh spoke to him as one speaks with a friend. When Moses found the courage to ask God the greatest favor, " 'Show me your glory,' Yahweh replied, 'I will let all my splendor pass in front of you, and I will pronounce before you the name Yahweh. . . . You cannot see my face, for man cannot see me and live.' And Yahweh said, 'Here is a place beside me. You must stand on the rock, and when my glory passes by, I will put you in a cleft of the rock and shield you with my hand while I pass by. Then I will take my hand away and you shall see the back of me, but you cannot see my face' " (Exodus 33:9-23).

The prophet Isaiah had a similar experience of God's purifying holiness (Isa. 6:5-8). In holy fear, he stood before God, Lord of the seraphim and cherubim, and cried, "I am lost for I am a man of unclean lips and live among a people of unclean lips, and my eyes have looked at the King, the Lord of Hosts." But then the prophet experienced the purifying fire of God's holiness. One of the seraphs took a glowing coal from the altar with tongs, and touched his mouth saying, "See now, this has touched your lips; your sin is taken away, your iniquity is purged." Then the prophet rejoiced and responded to God's calling, "Here I am, send me."

St. John of the Cross felt that a person not yet purified from inclination to sin would die if exposed even to the mystical vision experienced by Moses. God is holy Love, and a blissful light for those who are humble and sincere; but for others he is a purifying fire that pains and shocks.

To his friends God reveals himself gradually, cleansing them more and more from motives that are less than pure. If we gratefully accept the purifying fire of his holiness and his nearness, and commit ourselves to him with a trusting heart and profound sorrow for our sins, then we are approaching the blissful experience of the beatitude, "they shall see God."

Some young people today have a foolish dream that drugs can give them a deeper spiritual experience without the patient effort of conversion to God and neighbor; but the true God-experience can be known only by those who undergo the necessary purification from all selfishness and pride.

In an ancient manuscript of St. Luke's Gospel, the second petition of the Our Father was not "Thy kingdom come" but "Let your Holy Spirit come upon us and cleanse us." Therefore, with the prophets and saints, we should pray, "Grant us, O Lord, a heart renewed; grant us a new spirit."

When our hearts are purified and we are guided by God's gracious love, our whole life becomes a glad response to him in the service of our fellowmen. There the kingdom of God is at hand. The sincerity of our prayer for a new heart and spirit must constantly be tested, however, by examining our motives, intentions and habits. We may be quite knowledgeable about objective principles and all the formulations of Christian ethics, but if our motives are self-seeking, we remain always outside the kingdom. We are entering the kingdom when we truly seek God with a pure heart, free from selfish intentions and ready to join with all people of good will in a sincere search for what is good, truthful and right. Then, in the concrete problems of life, we find the right solutions and put into practice what our conscience dictates.

Purity of heart is woefully lacking in anyone who asks, "If I do this, will it be a mortal or a venial sin?" The pure of heart approach decisions from a totally different direction. Guided by the grace of the Spirit, they ask, "How can I render thanks to the Lord for all he has given me? How can I become more worthy of the love with which God has loved me?''

A sincere conscience is the test of purity of heart. The Second Vatican Council described conscience as "the most secret core and sanctuary of a man. There he is alone with God; His voice echoes in his depths.'' It is possible for a sincere conscience to err, but moral evil can be imputed only when a conscience is insincere. There is moral evil also if anyone tries to manipulate another person's conscience.

If we have a specifically Christian conscience, we examine all our thoughts, desires, words, deeds and omissions in the light of the Eucharist, rendering thanks to the Father for having given us our light and our truth in Jesus Christ, and giving thanks to Christ who has given himself for us on the cross.

When we adore God in spirit and truth, we find the proper criterion for each of our decisions, and choose only what can be offered to God, our Father, as an expression of thanksgiving for all he has done for us. If our hearts are filled with that love of God which Christ has revealed to us, then we can trustfully hope for the beatitude promised for those ''whose hearts are pure.''

SOCIAL DIMENSION

It would be a serious mistake to think of purity of heart as only a private, personal matter. While it is indeed essential for personal growth and eternal beatitude, it is equally essential for building a more fraternal and more equitable world.

What is most lacking in today's world is the mutual trust that can be established only through purity of motives. Those who have forgotten God, the Father of all, and Christ, the servant of all, seek first their own power, career, title or promotion while professing service for the common good. But those who abide with Christ, the Servant, truly work for the good of all and build up, by their purity of heart, the mutual trust so necessary for a peaceful and humane society and world.

If in all that we do we are helping to create a social climate in which sincerity and mutual trust are possible, then we are acquiring a pure heart. We think especially of Christians called to the vocations of educator, journalist, lawyer, doctor, politician. If they create a climate of trust and truthfulness, they are authentic builders of community. A society is civilized, truly human and redeemed if its members can trust the sincerity of one another and especially of those in positions of influence and authority.

We can rejoice that most of today's youth sets high priority on honesty, the sincerity of words and actions, and sincerity of purpose. It is a gift of the Lord of history if we begin to ask ourselves if our motives are upright, and to examine whether our words and actions are really communicating truth.

Purity of intention and absolute sincerity in communication are indispensable for those who have dedicated their lives to the service of the Gospel and the promotion of human dignity. For someone to attempt to help the cause of religion by half-truths is, in fact, a form of unbelief. We cannot witness to the eternal truth of God's loving and saving presence if we have not purified our motives and have not learned to be trustworthy in our communication and all our dealings. "Again, you have learned that our forefathers were told, 'Do not break your oath,' and, 'Oaths sworn to the Lord must be kept.' But what I tell you is this: . . . Plain 'Yes' or 'No' is all you

need to say; anything beyond that comes from the devil'' (Matt. 5:33-37).

Formerly, in a Church plagued by distrust, we professors of theology had to swear an oath against Modernism once or twice a year. Under such circumstances, one can imagine how the spirit of careerism, promises of promotions and threats of discrimination could undermine sincerity and trustworthiness. We can hope that a transition from the Constantinian era to a faith of personal choice will help us to understand better the requirements of the Sermon on the Mount.

A strange kind of moralism used to think only of chastity when the word ''purity'' was mentioned. Of course, chastity also belongs to purity, but only if all human relationships are marked by mutual respect and sincerity can sexuality follow the same rule. For the ''pure of heart'' there will then be no untrue declarations of love and no manipulation of others. Rigid moral norms and threats of mortal sin cannot achieve what genuine sincerity and purity of motivation can.

Pavlov and Skinner, the experts of brainwashing and manipulation techniques, hold that people can and should be manipulated through a conditioning process based on fear of sanction and hope of reward. But people who do not transcend the immediate incentives of reward and punishment become defenseless objects of all kinds of manipulation. One who seeks only praise, promotion and success for himself will inevitably be a manipulated manipulator, unable to make progress in true freedom or to grow in the knowledge of a loving God.

To experience true freedom and inner peace, and to ''see God'': these greatest of gifts are reserved for those whose hearts are pure.

Eternal Father, let your Holy Spirit come upon us and cleanse us. Purify our hearts so that we may know you and serve you who are purity and holiness of love.

Father, we all speak of freedom, boast of freedom, cry for freedom. We thank you for having taught us, through your son Jesus Christ, how to set out for true liberation. By loving you and learning from Our Lord, your Son and Servant, how to serve our brothers and sisters with pure intention, we shall find the way to true liberty. Give us perseverence, Lord, so that we may go up the Mount with Jesus to listen to his words and to learn from him who is, like you, absolute purity of love, of justice and of peace.

HOW BLEST ARE THE PEACEMAKERS; GOD SHALL CALL THEM HIS CHILDREN

CHRIST, THE PRINCE OF PEACE

In faith we gather around Jesus, acknowledging him as the Son of God, the Messiah, and as the Prince of Peace promised by the prophet. "For there is a child born for us, a son given to us, and dominion is laid on his shoulders; and this is the name they give him . . . Prince of Peace. Wide is his dominion in a peace that has no end" (Isa. 9:5-7).

Christ's birth was heralded by the angels' song, "Glory to God in the highest heaven, and on earth peace among men of good will" (Luke 2:14). The angels' welcome spelled out also his mission. He was sent to bring glory to God by bringing peace to earth.

The peace Christ came to establish on earth is the messianic peace of salvation and liberation. On the Mount of the Beatitudes he shares with us, by the power of the Holy Spirit, both his peace and his mission. His word is *Shalom*.

There is no other word in the Old Testament that is so full of promise as the word *Shalom*. It includes all the promises of the messianic age. But to bring this peace to earth, Jesus paid the highest price in the blood of the new and everlasting covenant through which we are all brothers and sisters in him, the eternal Son of the Father.

Jesus spoke the word and lived it; he brought peace with him wherever he went. And after he had suffered for peace and died that we might share in it, the risen Lord greeted his disciples with *Shalom!* and they were filled with joy. They not only received the word of reconciliation and the good news about peace; in faith they received him who *is* Peace. By opening their hearts to the Prince of Peace, they recognized and honored him as the Son of God. Thus they received the mission which now, in our own day, is ours: to proclaim peace, and to be witnesses and ministers to universal reconciliation.

PEACEMAKERS WITH CHRIST

When we gather around Christ on the Mount, it is to receive from him reconciliation and peace; and by experiencing this peace, we come to know how precious it is. But we can be called sons and daughters of God only if we accept the gift with such gratitude that it becomes our mission in life to be channels of the messianic peace for others.

If, in faith, we truly understand what it means to be called sons and daughters of the holy God, then we shall pray with St. Francis,

"Lord, make me an instrument of thy peace." And if we are sincere in this prayer, we shall develop all those qualities necessary for an ambassador of Christ's peace: readiness to serve with him as servant of all; compassion for victims, the needy, sinners; a spirit of gentleness and nonviolence; a pure heart that desires nothing more than to help our brother to find peace and justice through Christ.

We cannot, however, share with others what we do not have ourselves. Therefore we have to maintain peace in our own hearts and minds in order to proclaim it effectively. The closer we gather around Christ, the more we abide with him who is the Prince of Peace, the more we appreciate our mission as peacemakers.

Shalom is God's gift and a gift of amazing consequence. It changes completely our relationships with God our Father, with our Lord and Brother Jesus Christ, with our neighbor, the whole world around us, and especially with ourselves. Messianic peace means that we are accepted by God as his children, and when we realize that the holy God accepts us as we are, we can accept ourselves and even bear a part of our neighbor's burden.

God meets us where we are in order to lead us to the fullness of our dignity as his children. Knowing this, we see ourselves and our lives in a totally different light. And in this light, we can grow to the full stature of sons and daughters of God.

SOCIAL DIMENSION

While we think gratefully about the peace of heart and mind that Christ grants us, and the new relationship with God that allows us to accept ourselves, we cannot forget the social implications of our mission to be instruments and ambassadors of his peace.

Jesus came to reconcile all people with the Father and among themselves. If we are to serve the Prince of Peace, then like him we have to bring peace and promote it wherever we go, in whatever realm of life we touch. Christ's peace is an indivisible entity; we cannot seize only a piece of it. We cannot be wholly at peace ourselves unless we share the same beatitude with others. When we open ourselves in gratitude to this gift of the Lord, we also accept our mission to carry it with us to our nextdoor neighbor and into our whole community. It was for the whole world's peace that Christ came.

We think first of peace in the family. The sacrament of marriage can be lived in such a way that husband and wife become signs of God's presence for each other and for their children. Where there is love in the home, mutual respect and a readiness to ask for and graciously to grant forgiveness, there will be the peace of Christ.

We think also of religious communities and of the whole Church. What horrible contradiction it is when those who sign themselves as disciples of the Prince of Peace indulge in harmful quarrels in the name of his mission! Rigorists who think more about words in a law book than about Christ's words in the beatitudes will never become messengers of his peace.

How we deal with polarization in religious communities and in the Church at large is relevant to our mission of peace. In a time of cultural upheaval and Church renewal, tension and polarization are inevitable. Christians are a part of their culture and their time. But we can accept diversity of opinion in our communities and in the various parts of the church while, at the same time, respecting each other and continuing a fruitful dialogue in which we learn and unlearn. We can express our convictions gently yet effectively. We can sometimes offer our opinions as questions rather than theses,

and thus not only promote harmonious discussion but invite more thoughtful consideration of our view than it might otherwise receive.

Messianic peace includes, of necessity, social justice and peace. The authentic peacemaker has a passionate interest in peace and justice for all people and nations, with special attention toward the poorer ones. Progress in this political field depends to a considerable extent on an enlightened public opinion which influences political decisions. Hence, a part of our energies should be dedicated to this field. A group of American nuns has already embraced this opportunity to serve the Prince of Peace by becoming especially well informed about key social issues and their relation to politics, with the intention of arousing the social consciences of politicians. Our votes are important here. No one who wants to follow the Prince of Peace will ever promote or defend unjust economic, social or political positions, or vote for representatives who promote or defend them.

Working for peace, we must work *in* peace, with genuine respect for those who sincerely think differently from us. As peacemakers, we cannot allow ourselves to make broad negative judgments about groups or individuals. Not only do such judgments sin against truth and justice but also against our mission.

The Eucharistic celebration unites people of the most diverse backgrounds and viewpoints. If we accept each other and truly gather around Christ, the Prince of Peace, the community of faith will surely have its impact on every field and phase of life in the world.

There is no greater joy than to be called sons and daughters of God and to be invited by Jesus to follow him in his mission for peace on earth. This joy is surely one of the most powerful forces in the world; it can affect the whole future of human society. The mission of peace and of justice in peace is not a task imposed from without; it arises from within anyone who truly believes in the Gospel. For whoever believes in Jesus Christ, who is Peace Incarnate, believes also in the possibility of peace among men and among nations. If it is possible, then we cannot excuse ourselves from actively sharing in the effort to achieve it.

Jesus Christ, our Lord and our Brother, by your zeal to unite all people you have revealed the Father to us and made us deeply conscious that we are all children of the same Father, brothers and sisters of one another.

Send us your Spirit so that our lives may bear fruit in love, joy and peace. Make us so grateful for the gift of your Shalom *that we can accept the sometimes difficult task of being messengers to others of your peace. Never allow us to forget the price you paid, so that we too will be ready to pay whatever price is necessary.*

Forgive us our sins of envy, jealousy, and all sins against the honor and dignity of our brothers and sisters, or whatever diminishes fraternal harmony. Make us aware of the source of many of these sins. Is it that we have failed to go up the Mount of the Beatitudes with you? Or, if we did meditate and pray, did we forget that you came for the multitude?

Help us to preserve peace in all the situations of life. Grant us the joy of the Gospel so that, with you and through you, we can radiate peace, goodness and benevolence to those around us.

HOW BLEST ARE THOSE WHO HAVE SUFFERED PERSECUTION FOR THE CAUSE OF RIGHT; THE KINGDOM OF HEAVEN IS THEIRS

CHRIST, THE KINGDOM OF HEAVEN

The eighth beatitude concludes with the same marvelous promise as the first: ''The kingdom of heaven is theirs.'' The kingdom of heaven means the realm of God, the domain where God reigns as king. In Jesus himself God reigns supreme; the heavenly kingdom is in him.

He came to do the Father's will, not his own. Rejecting the

temptation to be the powerful Messiah whom many wanted, he came as Yahweh's Servant, and suffered so that gentleness, mercy, justice and peace might prevail in the hearts of men, and God might reign on earth as in heaven. The lesson of the beatitudes is therefore the same as that of the Paschal Mystery; the Mount of the Beatitudes and Mount Calvary are one.

We come together, then, around Christ who died for us, has risen for us, and wants to continue his mission through disciples who can credibly proclaim the beatitudes: disciples who believe that they can live the Gospel and who want to live it regardless of the cost. In our midst is the Blessed One who has suffered persecution for the cause of right.

Christ is the Prophet who brings the entire history of the prophets to its culmination. He scourges the conscience of the rich and mighty, the privileged classes, and especially the religious hypocrites who set aside God's law of love with pious words and enforce burdensome traditions in his name.

Had Christ restricted his ministry to offering personal peace of mind without addressing himself to the burning problems of life in community and of social justice, he would not have unmasked the abuses and alienations in organized religion and ultimately would not have suffered persecution by political and religious leaders of his time.

Christ, the Prophet, is the perfect monotheist. He lives wholly in relationship with the one God and Father of all, and stirs up in us that faith in one God which makes us want to unite all men and nations in justice and peace. Christ paid the highest price for his prophetic vocation, but his willingness to pay it clearly indicates to his disciples that those who receive the charism of prophet will have to follow him.

This beatitude, proclaimed by the Prophet to all who share his vocation and mission, sheds a new light on the concept of "original sin." Jesus' teaching puts little emphasis on the Adam who committed the first sin by refusing to do the good he could have done and yielding to the evil he could have avoided. Rather, he emphasizes the solidarity of sin in a world of closed-mindedness, group arrogance and abuse of religion and power. The history of the sin of the world can be read in the sufferings of all the prophets, and eventually in the repudiation of Christ by the religious leaders who sent him to die on Calvary.

This sin of the world continues, and so does the suffering of the prophets who challenge the political leaders and Church authorities who, by their blindness, inertia and alienation, block the coming of God's kingdom to the people of our own time.

Centuries before the coming of Christ, Plato wrote, "If the perfect and just man were to appear, this evil world would crucify him." Christ is just, the Holy One sent from heaven. His very holiness is what challenges the self-righteous and arrogant whose power and privilege is at stake. Yet that holiness is also what appeals most forcefully to his disciples, inspiring them to turn and follow him in wholehearted commitment to the heavenly Father's justice on earth.

GATHERED AROUND CHRIST, THE PROPHET

Whoever, in faith, has truly met Jesus, the Prophet, will be mindful of the crowd. And whoever loves Christ's Church will therefore sometimes face the unpleasant duty of protesting the attitudes and actions of those who have not kept themselves open to the joys and hopes, the needs and the anguish of the people of God.

In her history, the Church would have fulfilled her role better in the world if, in times of corruption and infidelity to the Gospel, there had been more prophetic courage to unmask and oppose the evils. Instead, blind obedience, slavish submission and even careerist diplomacy dictated a silence that connived in the infidelities.

Men and women with a prophetic charism are not readymade saints; they have their own faults and weaknesses which often make them especially vulnerable to the criticisms, misunderstandings and defamation they must endure. But a keen awareness of their own failings also enters into the perspective of the beatitudes. It can make them even more humble and unselfish in fulfilling their mission. Mindful of their own sins and shortcomings, and remembering that Christ died for them, accepting the suffering inherent in his mission, they are not overwhelmed by contradiction. Their inner peace remains undisturbed, and they can leave it to others to discern whether or not they manifest the fruits of the Spirit: joy, peace, kindness, benevolence, goodness, gentleness and self-control.

SOCIAL DIMENSION

The social dimension of active witness and suffering by those who follow Christ is obvious, and the promise that whoever suffers for the cause of right will share the heavenly kingdom further extends this social horizon.

To belong to the heavenly kingdom is to be under the reign of God and of his messenger, Jesus Christ. Believers in the universal Lordship of God will do their best, always and everywhere, to make this visible and effective in their families, their churches, their communities, and in whatever economic, cultural and political spheres of life they touch.

Political theology has shown that all religious attitudes and decisions have their impact on the life of society. An individualistic approach in religion, which fails to activate the yeast of the Gospel, introduces a harmful individualistic mentality in all realms of life. An overemphasis on obedience and conformity, and a one-sided insistence on priestly privilege in certain periods of Church history, have proven damaging for both the Church and society. But whenever the life of the Church reflects Christ, the Prophet, and wherever many people are ready to follow him and to suffer for the cause of right, there the Church remains the salt of the earth.

Action for the cause of right has a social bearing even when it does not meet with success. As Christians, we believe in the social fruitfulness of suffering for righteousness. Christ redeemed us on the cross and showed us that the way to a better world is through the power of unselfish love. The suffering of the apostles and of all those committed to justice and peace completes, in the life of Christ's disciples, the Paschal Mystery.

Throughout history men and women have suffered often seemingly in vain for the cause of right; but slowly, fitfully, through their cumulative efforts, mankind has advanced toward a more humane world. Yet even today thousands of Christ's followers and believers in one God and Father of all continue to suffer for the right in all parts of the world. Peter, who thrice denied Christ to save himself from suffering, tells us how he came to see later what suffering in the fellowship of Christ meant: "My dear friends, do not be bewildered by the fiery ordeal that is upon you, as though it were something extraordinary. It gives you a share in Christ's suffering, and that is cause for joy; and when his glory is revealed, your joy will be triumphant" (1 Peter 4:12-14).

Not only secular but also Church history give us examples of prophetic men and women who have suffered discrimination and even excommunication in the cause of right. Today the Church venerates certain saints who, during their lifetime, had much to suffer under a Church authority that failed to respond to their prophetic message. Others, though not canonized, are recognized as prophetic pioneers. Cardinal Newman and many others have given radiant witness of their fidelity to the Gospel and to the Church in the midst of machinations and opposition.

Love of neighbor and adoration of God call us today to be interested in political life. To make our contribution toward freedom from the age-old slavery of war, terrorism, and from various types of exploitation, we have to put aside our own interests and work for the common good. We must realize, however, that specific commitment to public life at any level requires high competence, discernment and the courage to suffer for the cause of right.

Here again it is most important that we stay close to Christ, pondering his word, being guided by his Spirit. Woe to priests, religious, lay apostles and Christian politicans who never know contradiction and never suffer the anger of opposing groups! Whoever has the courage to live the Gospel and to suffer for the cause of right will be, like Christ, "destined for the fall and the rising of many . . . destined to be a sign that is rejected" (Luke 2:34). Helder Camara's option for solidarity with the poor has forced many people to rethink their positions. Pope John provoked violent opposition from those who were concerned more for their security than for reform of the Church. This was undoubtedly one of his great sufferings.

Lord Jesus Christ, we adore you who so perfectly embodies the Father's kingdom. We praise you as the Prophet and as the one who showed us the meaning of faith in one God, the Father. You brought to completion the history of all the prophets before you, and plainly told your disciples that they must share your suffering if they are truly to stand for the cause of right.

Lord, make us know your name as Prophet, and honor it by our whole life. Send us your Spirit that we may truthfully believe in him who has spoken and still continues to speak through your prophets today; and give us the sincerity to listen to the discomforting prophets who awaken us from our inertia and superficiality.

Lord, give us strength to live the Gospel even when those around us urge on us a false prudence in order to avoid all contradiction and suffering. Fill us, Lord, with that inner strength and joy that will enable us to continue to work for the cause of right, no matter what the cost.

LIGHT
FOR ALL THE WORLD

CHRIST IS THE LIGHT

Nine times our Lord introduces his teaching on the Mount with, "How blest. . . ." Then he turns to his disciples and gives them their mission: "You are salt to the world. And if the salt becomes tasteless, how is its saltiness to be restored? It is now good for nothing but to be thrown away and trodden underfoot. You are light for all the world. A town that stands on a hill cannot be hidden. When a lamp is lit, it is not put under the meal-tub but on the lampstand, where it gives light to everyone in the house. And you, like the lamp, must shed light among your fellows, so that when they see the good you do, they may give praise to your Father in heaven" (Matt. 5:13-16).

This teaching leaves no doubt that the moral imperative of the Sermon on the Mount is one with the Gospel. Christ himself is the Gospel and the Way. He is the salt and the light for all the world. And he gives his disciples their mission by giving them a share in his own life, his joy, his light, to carry to the ends of the earth.

[99]

Christ, the eternal Word of God and his visible image, is the perfect sacrament of salvation. We, too, with his whole Church are called to be sacraments, visible signs of God who is Love, Mercy, Peace and Justice. Insofar as we follow Christ in all his ways, giving honor to him, and through him to the Father, we are making Christ visible to those around us and are thus sacraments to the world.

The Good News, "You are the light for all the world," continues the wonderful words of creation when "God said, 'Let there be light,' and there was light, and God saw that the light was good, and he separated light from darkness" (Gen. 1:3-4). The prologue to the Gospel of St. John complements this song of creation: "When all things began, the Word already was. The Word dwelt with God, and what God was, the Word was. . . . All that came to be was alive with his life, and that life was the light of men. The light shines on in the dark, and the darkness has never quenched it" (John 1:1-5).

Not only in words but by his whole life, Jesus tells us, "I am the light of the world. No follower of mine shall wander in the dark; he shall have the light of life" (John 8:12). The sun that lights our daily rounds is but a pale symbol of the Light that came into the world to guide us on the way of salvation. "I have come into the world as light so that no one who has faith in me should remain in darkness" (John 12:46). Coming not for his own glory but to reveal the splendor of the Father, Christ shines upon us, lighting the way to our Father's kingdom.

Christ is salt to the world; he gives savor to everything. Without him our days are flavorless; with him they taste of delight. And just as salt gives taste to the food by giving itself instead of preserving itself, so Christ gives himself wholly, so that we all may have life, joy and peace.

YOU ARE LIGHT

Our dignity and mission as disciples can only be understood by turning to Christ, the source of our life and light.

Christ does not begin his sermon with "You must" or "You shall." He sings the most magnificent canticle of the sun, the Light that shines for all of us to show the Way, the Truth, the Life. He does not send us on our mission to be "light for the world" until he teaches us that we must first receive everything—truth, grace and light—from him.

This, then, is the real foundation of Christian morality. St. Paul explains it well. "Though you were once all darkness, now as Christians you are light. Live like men who are at home in daylight, for where light is, there all goodness springs up, all justice and truth" (Eph. 5:8-9). "Awake, sleeper, rise from the dead, and Christ will shine upon you" (Eph. 5:14). He tells the Thessalonians: "You are all children of light, children of day" (1 Thess. 5:5). And Christ himself speaks of his disciples as "children of the light" (Luke 16:8), although they will be fully enlightened only when they are totally converted to him.

The dynamism of Christian morality is not only in the imperative "Let your light shine," but even more in the Good News proclaimed by Jesus and written in our hearts by the Holy Spirit: "You are light." Whoever accepts the Good News with faith, trust and gratitude realizes that his mission arises from an inner call of grace to be truthful to one's own name and to live the new life in the light of the Lord.

Light is a symbol of purity. Jesus asks purity of heart and of intention to let our light shine out to others. This does not at all contradict another invitation from Christ: "When you pray, go into a room by yourself, shut the door, and pray to your Father who is there in the secret place" (Matt. 6:6). We cannot be a light that turns the eyes of others to the Father if any part of our intention is to make a display of our religion or to advance our own interests. Only if we are aware that God is the source of all good and, in thanksgiving, we want to bring all glory to the name of the Father, can we truly be "salt for the earth" and "light for the world."

We see, then, that the morality of the beatitudes is the morality of the Paschal Mystery. Jesus himself is the light that does not lose its splendor when it enters the darkness of Golgotha. By the words of the beatitudes, by the example of his whole life, and even more by the Paschal Mystery, Christ teaches us that "Whoever cares for his own safety is lost; but if a man will let himself be lost for my sake and for the Gospel, that man is safe" (Mark 8:34). "Whoever seeks his life selfishly loses his true self; whoever gives his life for my sake finds his true self" (Matt. 10:39).

By surrendering himself on the cross, Christ gives witness to his utter trust in the Father, and the Father glorifies him. So will those who believe in the Paschal Mystery, and serve their fellowmen in the name of the Lord, know that they will find their true selves and the fullness of life and light when they follow Jesus who came into the world to light the way.

SOCIAL DIMENSION

The beatitudes are like a canticle of joy sung for all the world. With each beatitude, and especially with the final message, "You are light for all the world," Christ sends us on our mission with thankful hearts. He came to be Savior of the world and Servant to the world, and he has taken us up the Mount of the Beatitudes in view of the crowd, to teach us how to be witnesses to his Gospel by being servants of our brethren and peacemakers wherever we are.

Grateful acceptance of the Good News, and of all the gifts God has given us, spells out our mission to share everything with others. It is a matter of God's justice that we make good use of our talents by concern, love and service for our brothers and sisters. Christ tells us this when he warns that "If the salt becomes tasteless, it is good for nothing but to be thrown away and trodden underfoot" (Matt. 5:13).

To be a disciple of Christ without being ready to share the joy of faith with others and to be servant for the common good is a contradiction. One cannot be salt and not serve as salt. How can we savor the lives of others if we selfishly reserve the salt for ourselves? Having shared his light and truth with us, and having brought forth the new creation in us ("You are light for all the world"), Jesus points out the necessity to share. "And you must shed light among your fellows so that, when they see the good you do, they may give praise to your Father in heaven" (Matt. 5:16).

As long as we are true disciples of Christ, we are like a town standing on a hill. If we have living faith we are, by necessity, a living Gospel. Not only do we proclaim the Gospel of our Lord Jesus Christ but, above all, we live its message in the service of our neighbor and the world, so that we make known him who is the source of all that is good, truthful and beautiful.

A follower of Christ is open to all that is good in the world. Since he believes in the One who is source of all life and light, he honors God by honoring good wherever he finds it. Not to credit the good in others, of whatever faith or none, is to deny praise

to the Father of all, and to use selfishly the gifts God gave us is to steal the glory that belongs to God alone.

Where there is living faith, there is light and convincing witness and realization of one's personal mission. Like Jesus on the Mount of the Beatitudes, we should turn our eyes to the crowd. Who is in the crowd? Our family? Our community? Our fellow-citizens of mixed colors, creeds and classes? When we have gathered around Christ and found in him the source of joy and light, then we shall share his precious gifts with all for whom they were given.

To have a living faith and trust in the Lord is not to be blind to evil. Being light, we see our own faults first and look for the good in others, since all good comes from God. In the light of Christ we discover all the opportunities to serve God and neighbor, and to help others to discover in themselves the inner resources that come from God and lead to the fulness of light and life. Then they too will give praise to the Father.

Almighty God, Creator of heaven and earth, we believe that you are our Father and that you can make us children worthy of you as brothers and sisters who lead one another closer to you and walk in your light.

We believe that you have shared all your wisdom, your holiness and your love with your Son, your eternal Word. By sending him to be our brother, you have given us everything.

We believe in Jesus Christ, Light of Light, true God and true man. Through him and in him, we share in your own life.

We believe that you have called us into your light by sending us your Son and the Spirit of Truth. If we entrust ourselves to you and are guided by the Holy Spirit, we shall not walk in darkness but

will become for each other a humble light that points to you, the One who is Light of Light.

Father, we praise you for having glorified your Servant, Jesus Christ, who gave his life for his brethren. For all of us you made him the source of everlasting life. We thank you for having called us to abide in Christ and to be the salt of the earth and light for the world.

We believe in the Holy Spirit, the giver of life, who has spoken through Christ, the Prophet, and still speaks through his prophets. Help us to fulfill our mission to be a sign of your loving presence for all in need. Help us to live our baptism and to give witness to Jesus Christ who was baptized in water, in the Spirit, and in his blood.

God, our Father, make us firm in hope. May we live in communion with the saints in saving solidarity, striving all together toward a new earth and a new heaven.

Help us, Lord, to be salt to the earth and light for the world. Help us to serve you with a pure heart so that all who see the sincerity of our service may praise you, Father, with the Son and the Holy Spirit, now and forever. Amen!